Football Poetry Memory Book: Brown and Orange Edition

Football Poetry Memory Book: Brown and Orange Edition

Walter the Educator

Silent King Books
a WhichHead Entertainment Imprint

Copyright © 2024 by Walter the Educator

All rights reserved. No part of this book may be reproduced in any manner whatsoever without written permission except in the case of brief quotations embodied in critical articles and reviews.

First Printing, 2024

Disclaimer

This book is a literary work; the story is not about specific persons, teams, games, locations, situations, and/or circumstances unless mentioned in a historical context. Any resemblance to real persons, teams, games, locations, situations, and/or circumstances is coincidental. This book is for entertainment and informational purposes only. The author and publisher offer this information without warranties expressed or implied. No matter the grounds, neither the author nor the publisher will be accountable for any losses, injuries, or other damages caused by the reader's use of this book. The use of this book acknowledges an understanding and acceptance of this disclaimer.

Football Poetry Memory Book: Brown and Orange Edition is a memory book that belongs to the Sports Poetry Memory Book Series by Walter the Educator. Collect them all and more books at WaltertheEducator.com.

USE THE EXTRA SPACE TO DOCUMENT YOUR FOOTBALL MEMORIES THROUGHOUT THE YEARS

This little collectible keepsake book belongs to

_____

Beneath the sky, where autumn calls,

A battle rages, football's brawl.

With hearts of fire, bold and strange,

They charge the field in Brown and Orange.

The Brown, like earth beneath their feet,

Solid, strong, with no retreat.

It whispers tales of grit and might,

Of warriors forged in endless fight.

Like soil that roots the mighty oak,

It bears the weight of every stroke.

In Brown, the strength of days gone by,

Where sweat and toil refuse to die.

And Orange, the fire that lights the way,

A flash of dawn in the light of day.

It burns like leaves in autumn's flame,

A beacon bright in football's name.

The Orange blazes wild and bold,

A sunset's kiss that never grows old.

It's energy, it's passion's scream,

The pulse behind each player's dream.

Together, Brown and Orange blend,

A union where the lines extend.

Like sunset fading into night,

They carry forward through the fight.

The Brown, the backbone, never bends,

And Orange, the fire that transcends.

They work in tandem, stride by stride,

Each play, each pass, a rising tide.

In every jersey, every cleat,

These colors march with steady beat.

Brown, the anchor, Orange, the spark,

They carve their names into the dark.

A team that rises, never falls,

They answer when the whistle calls.

Through muddy fields and skies of gray,

In Brown and Orange, they make their way.

The Brown, like leather worn with pride,

A history no storm can hide.

It's in the grid of every face,

The marks of time that never erase.

The Orange, like fire in the soul,

A flash of spirit that takes control.

ABOUT THE CREATOR

Walter the Educator is one of the pseudonyms for Walter Anderson. Formally educated in Chemistry, Business, and Education, he is an educator, an author, a diverse entrepreneur, and he is the son of a disabled war veteran. "Walter the Educator" shares his time between educating and creating. He holds interests and owns several creative projects that entertain, enlighten, enhance, and educate, hoping to inspire and motivate you. Follow, find new works, and stay up to date with Walter the Educator™

at WaltertheEducator.com

Milton Keynes UK
Ingram Content Group UK Ltd.
UKHW020937041024
449263UK00011B/568